my itty-bitty bio

Sally Ride

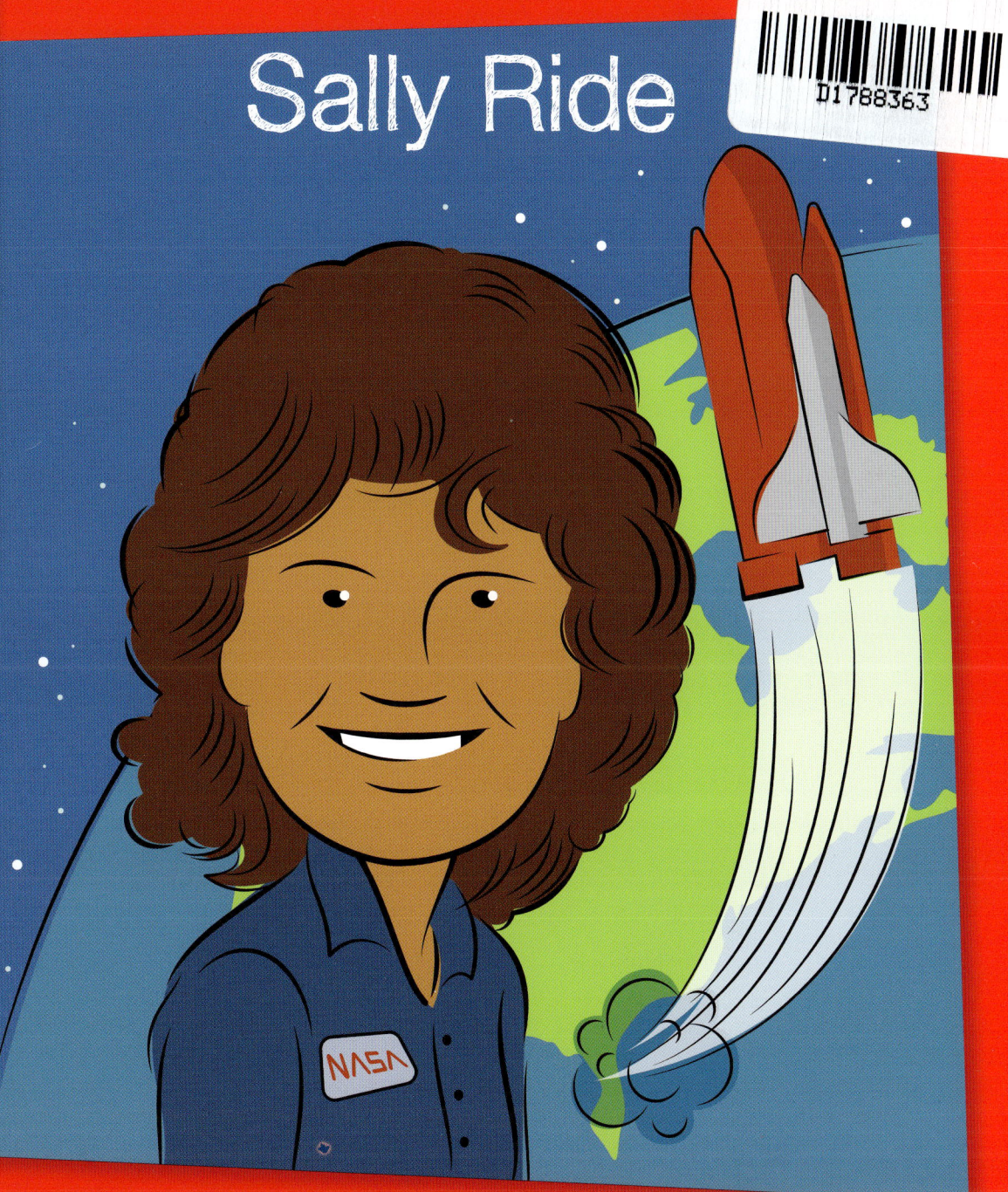

Published in the United States of America by Cherry Lake Publishing
Ann Arbor, Michigan
www.cherrylakepublishing.com

Content Adviser: Ryan Emery Hughes, Doctoral Student, School of Education, University of Michigan
Reading Adviser: Marla Conn MS, Ed., Literacy specialist, Read-Ability, Inc.
Book Design: Jennifer Wahi
Illustrator: Jeff Bane

Photo Credits: © haveseen/Shutterstock, 5; © jejim/Shutterstock, 7; © NASA, 9; © NASA, 11; © NASA, 13; © NASA, 15, 22; © NASA Langley Research Center, 17; © NASA, 19, 23; © NASA, 21; Cover, 6, 12, 16, Jeff Bane; Various frames throughout, © Shutterstock Images

Copyright ©2018 by Cherry Lake Publishing
All rights reserved. No part of this book may be reproduced or utilized in any form or by any means without written permission from the publisher.

Library of Congress Cataloging-in-Publication Data

Names: Loh-Hagan, Virginia, author. | Bane, Jeff, 1957- illustrator.
Title: Sally Ride / by Virginia Loh-Hagan ; [illustrator, Jeff Bane].
Other titles: My itty-bitty bio.
Description: Ann Arbor, MI : Cherry Lake Publishing, [2018] | Series: My
   itty-bitty bio | Audience: K to grade 3. | Includes index.
Identifiers: LCCN 2017030509| ISBN 9781534107090 (hardcover) | ISBN
   9781534108080 (pbk.) | ISBN 9781534109070 (pdf) | ISBN 9781534120068
   (hosted ebook)
Subjects: LCSH: Ride, Sally--Juvenile literature. | United States. National
   Aeronautics and Space Administration--Biography--Juvenile literature. |
   Women astronauts--United States--Biography--Juvenile literature. | Women
   physicists--United States--Biography--Juvenile literature.
Classification: LCC TL789.85.R53 L64 2018 | DDC 629.450092 [B] --dc23
LC record available at https://lccn.loc.gov/2017030509

Printed in the United States of America
Corporate Graphics

table of contents

My Story 4

Timeline 22

Glossary 24

Index 24

About the author: Dr. Virginia Loh-Hagan is an author, university professor, former classroom teacher, and curriculum designer. Like Sally Ride, she hopes girls keep reaching for the stars. She lives in San Diego with her very tall husband and very naughty dogs. To learn more about her, visit: www.virginialoh.com

About the illustrator: Jeff Bane and his two business partners own a studio along the American River in Folsom, California, home of the 1849 Gold Rush. When Jeff's not sketching or illustrating for clients, he's either swimming or kayaking in the river to relax.

my story

I was born in California. It was 1951.

I went to Stanford University.
I learned **science**.

What do you want to learn?

I saw an **ad**. **NASA** wanted women **astronauts**.

I got picked!

It was hard. Some people thought women weren't smart.

I trained. I flew jets. I learned more science.

I did two **missions**. I flew in space!

Do you want to fly in space?

I was the first American woman in space. I was also the youngest.

I was 32.

I used a **robot** arm. I grabbed things from space. That was my job.

I was the first woman to do this.

I became a teacher. I helped girls study science. I wrote books.

I planned fun science projects.

What science do you like to study?

I died in 2012. My dreams live on. I **inspire** others.

I reached for the stars. Others can, too!

What would you like to ask me?

timeline

1983

1950

↑
Born
1951

1987

2050

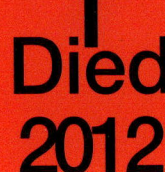

Died
2012

glossary & index

glossary

ad (AD) a public notice about jobs or goods being offered

astronauts (AS-truh-nawts) people who are trained to travel to space

inspire (in-SPYR) to fill someone with a feeling or an idea

missions (MISH-uhnz) journeys to space that have a purpose

NASA (NASS-uh) the National Aeronautics and Space Administration; it is in charge of the United States' space program

robot (ROH-baht) machine controlled by a computer

science (SYE-uhns) the study of nature and the world we live in

index

astronaut, 8, 12, 14, 16

birth, 4

California, 4, 6

robot, 16

science, 6, 12, 18

space, 8, 12, 14, 16

women, 8, 10, 14, 16, 18